OCEAN LIFE!

This Book Belongs to:

_____

OCEAN LIFE!

A Coloring and Activity Book for Kids

Jill Richardson

Illustrations by Kate Francis

ROCKRIDGE PRESS

WELCOME TO THE OCEAN!

Did you know that water covers more than half of the Earth? This water is called the ocean. Oceans are deep and wide and are home to many amazing sea creatures. There are way too many to count. Some are big and some are small. Some are colorful and some are not. Some have silly shapes and some do not. Some live near the surface of the water and some live on the bottom of the sea. There are so many things to learn about ocean animals!

Draw a picture of a big ocean animal:

Draw a picture of a small ocean animal:

Draw a picture of a colorful ocean animal:

Draw a picture of a silly-shaped ocean animal:

Before you begin exploring ocean animals,
let's see what you already know!

> **Draw a picture of your favorite ocean animal:**

> **Write or draw one thing you already know about an ocean animal:**

> **Write or draw one thing you would like to know about an ocean animal:**

Ready to find out about
some interesting ocean
animals? Let's begin
our fun!

ALL KINDS OF SHARKS

Many kinds of sharks swim in the oceans of our world. They come in different sizes, shapes, and colors. Sharks have amazing senses that help them track their prey. Can you find these sharks hidden in the puzzle? Look left to right, right to left, up and down, and diagonally.

Great White
Tiger Shark
Whale Shark

Hammerhead
Bull Shark
Nurse Shark

```
K R K M N X Y I G K B L D P T
R Y Z L G L K Q R H P L H I L
A H H I A O P A E F E E G Y X
H C L D O D H V A J A E Z D W
S R V M L S A K T Q R P Y K F
E C S O L R H E W S V J Z J U
S H L L V E C B H A Z Y D D R
R B U M H Y F A I R I Y L E Z
U B O A M M R L T U E J L V Y
N F L M J K X H E C A M S Y J
K R A H S E L A H W Y D M F Z
A K E D U U M C J M D F C A O
M V U H G W S P G K S W V P H
L Z A U Y N P X O H P A Y E C
K K A Z P N A I S V D U F E Y
```

See pages 66–69 for the answer key!

A sea otter likes to carry a rock wherever it goes
to crack open clams, shellfish, or crabs.

HUMPBACK WHALE'S A-MAZE-ING JOURNEY!

In the fall, humpback whales leave the cold waters of Alaska and swim to the warmer waters in Hawaii. They swim almost nonstop for several weeks. Help the humpback whale find the way to warmer water. Start at the ⭐ near Alaska and follow the maze to finish in Hawaii.

See pages 66–69 for the answer key!

If a sea star loses an arm, it can grow one back.

EXPLORE THE CORAL REEF

Many ocean animals swim in and around coral reefs. Most coral reefs grow in shallow waters in the ocean. You will find amazing animals under the water. There are **8** differences between these coral reef pictures. Can you find them all?

See pages 66–69 for the answer key!

The blue whale is the largest animal on Earth and can grow to almost 100 feet long. That's longer than three school buses!

This animal is called the "Unicorn of the Sea" because of the long tusk that sticks out of its head. Start at 1 and connect the dots to find out what animal this is.

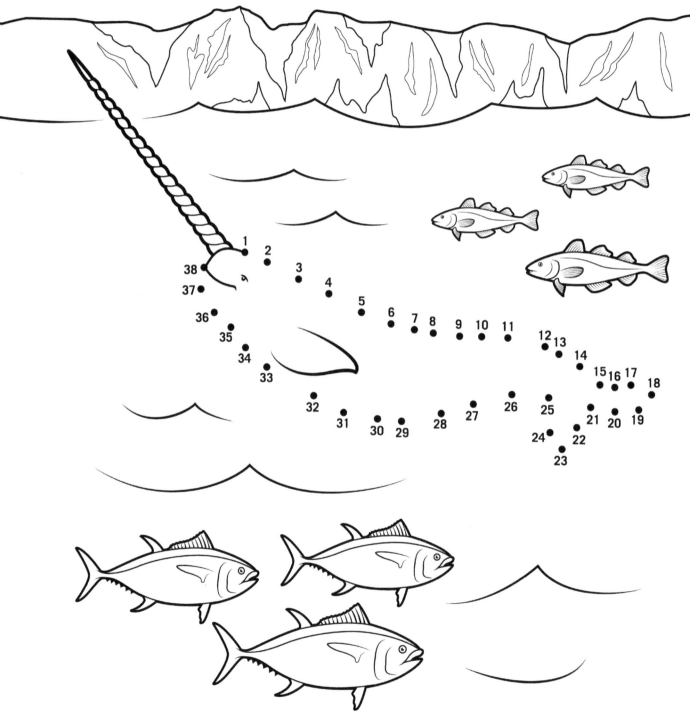

See pages 66–69 for the answer key!

A lobster sheds its shell when it grows—this is called "molting."

MARINE MAMMALS

Marine mammals have fur or hair, breathe air, and are warm-blooded. They also have live babies and feed them with milk. These things make them different from fish. Can you find these marine mammals? Look left to right, right to left, up and down, and diagonally.

Whale

Walrus

Manatee

Dolphin

Otter

Seal

Polar Bear

Porpoise

```
E W A L R U S I W W F J O E Y
J S R A E B R A L O P E T F U
T C I R Y S X V A I U E T L Q
I J D O E S Z Z U I S T E Q R
N R E A P D E N C D S A R J D
W N L M R R I Q X Q H N O Z I
R H E B S H O E Z X H A C P E
L A A X P L J P F N C M C N Q
B S H L R C E Q X B W Z L O Y
Y I O A E M B H O A H Z M Q O
J D A S G R E M O A S P N U T
S P C G Z N L C A E S Z P X G
A N E O H S A E S B S Q M N M
B B M P W O N A J A L T X O M
T V G K F X S D Y C G N C G H
```

A sea urchin has long spines that help protect it from its predators.

SEA TURTLE SCRAMBLE

Mother sea turtles dig nests on the beach to lay their eggs. Baby sea turtles called "hatchlings" come out of the eggs. At night they leave their nests and crawl to the ocean. Start at the ⭐ to help the baby sea turtles crawl from their sandy nests to the ocean waves.

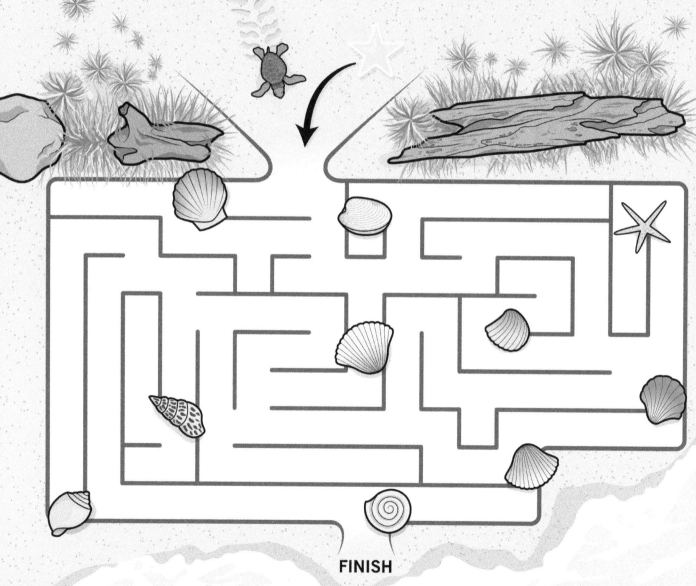

FINISH

 See pages 66–69 for the answer key!

A dolphin is not a fish.
It's a mammal that breathes
through its blowhole.

SEA LION COLONIES

Sea lions live in the ocean and on land. They like to rest together in groups called "colonies." Many times, you will find them soaking up the sun on rocks or swimming in the ocean together. There are **6** differences between these sea lion colonies. Can you find them all?

See pages 66–69 for the answer key!

A sunfish is the heaviest fish in the ocean. It can weigh up to 5,000 pounds—as much as a pickup truck.

This fish has slime on its skin to keep from getting cut or hurt on rocks. Start at 1 and connect the dots to find out what animal this is.

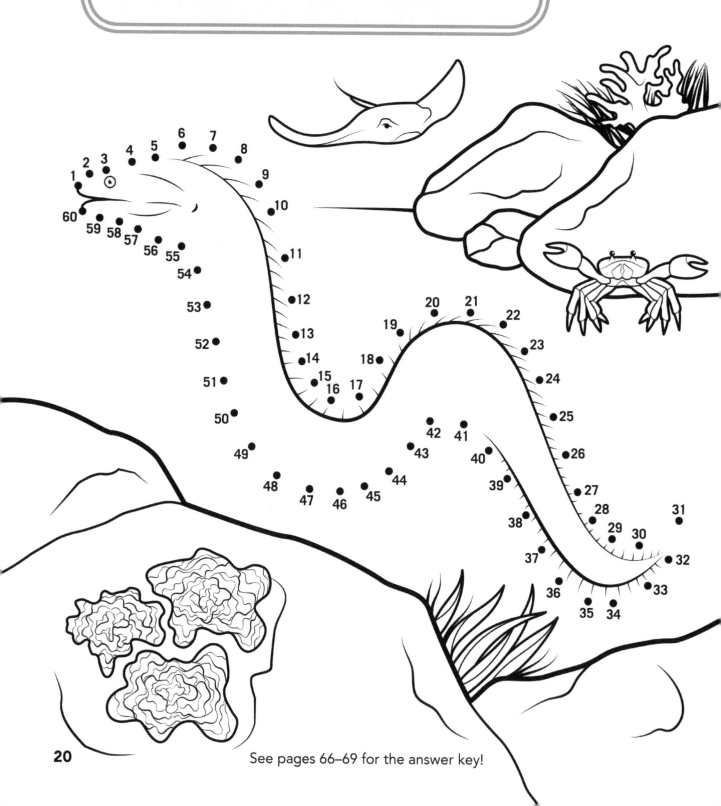

See pages 66–69 for the answer key!

An octopus can squirt ink, which keeps its enemies from harming it.

SINGING WHALES

Did you know that some whales can sing? They call to one another under the water. It sounds just like a song! Can you find these whales hidden in the puzzle? Look left to right, right to left, up and down, and diagonally.

Beluga

Blue Whale

Gray Whale

Humpback

Sperm Whale

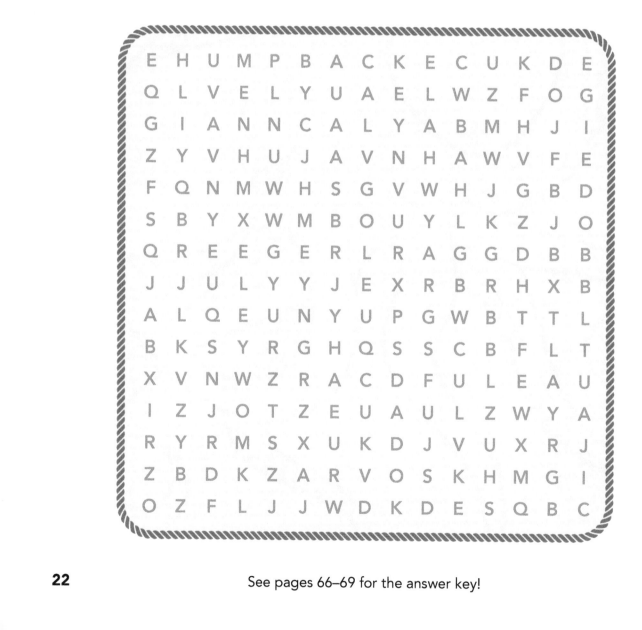

See pages 66–69 for the answer key!

A lionfish lives near coral reefs and hunts for food at night and early in the morning.

HERMIT CRAB'S HOME

A hermit crab finds a hard, empty shell for protection and shelter. As it grows, it swaps the smaller shell for a bigger one. Start at the ⭐ to help this hermit crab find a bigger shell.

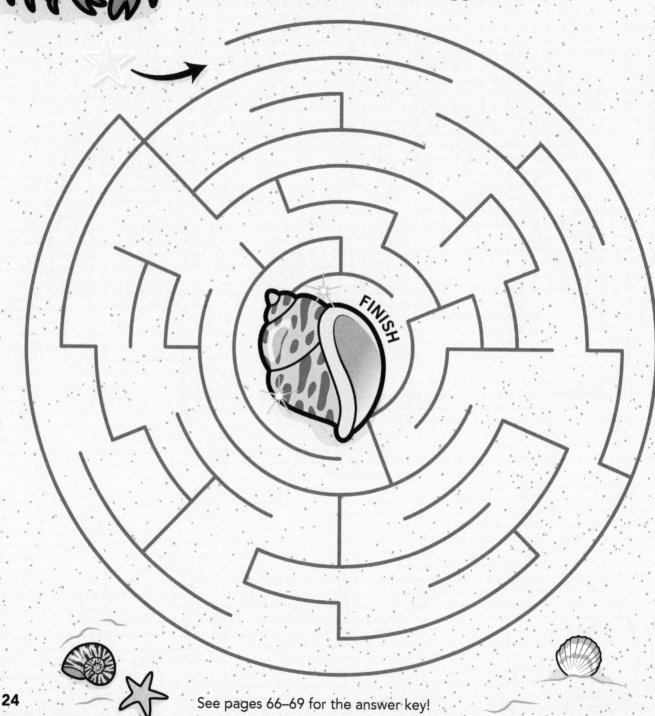

FINISH

See pages 66–69 for the answer key!

A sea slug is one of the most colorful animals in the ocean.

AN ENDANGERED OCEAN ANIMAL

The short-tailed albatross is in danger of becoming extinct. There are only around 2,200 left. Today their habitat is protected to help keep them safe. There are **5** differences between these pictures of short-tailed albatrosses. Can you find them all?

See pages 66–69 for the answer key!

To scare off its enemies, a pufferfish "puffs up" to twice its size.

This animal is an excellent fast swimmer. It has a long body that looks like a torpedo. Start at 1 and connect the dots to reveal the animals below.

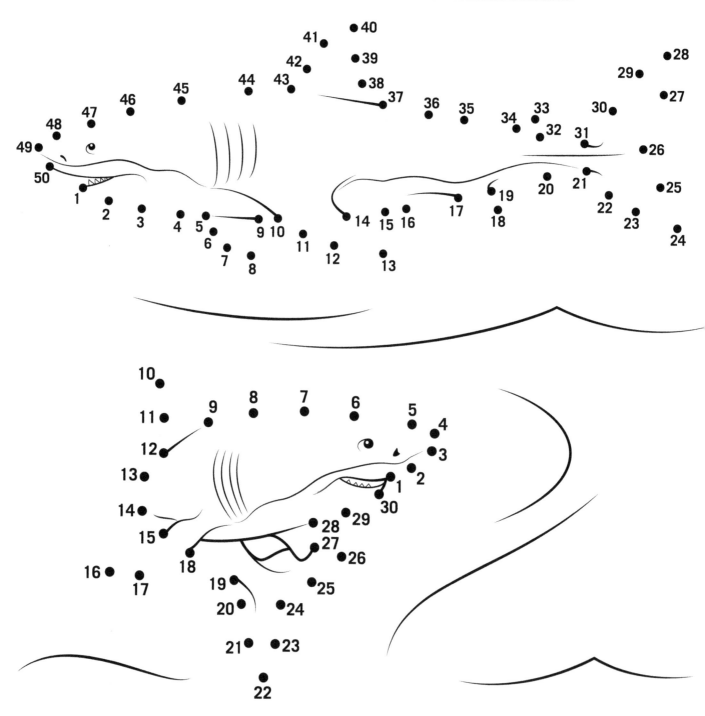

See pages 66–69 for the answer key!

A seal stays warm in cold water because it has a layer of fat under its skin called "blubber."

SAILING SEABIRDS

Seabirds eat fish and can drink salt water. They have two special glands on their heads to help get rid of the salt from the ocean water. Can you find these seabirds hidden in the puzzle? Look left to right, right to left, up and down, and diagonally.

Albatross   Seagull
Puffin   Loon
Penguin   Tern
Pelican   Murre

```
N P W W I T K E W D R L P Y V
A I Y A L J M T B S L R K W O
C J U T C L E H N U C Q O M G
I C J G S R Y H G M S F F V P
L D Z E N S F A I K K E O S Y
E U Q D T E E L B Q P D Y J U
P V Q G M S P O C X J I A C D
K Z P O O M P O L N A A J O O
Q D K U T K E N G Q N T X Q T
L U J R S I C R G D O B K B S
Z S K M F Y P N R M R M J X Y
D H Q J U K I K S S Q A Q W K
E C A U R R S X E U W J N W N
D F E S S O R T A B L A T W U
G G K K C C F E C P U F F I N
```

A sand dollar is purple, brown, or reddish purple and lives on the sandy seafloor.

FEEDING FRENZY

Blue marlin are fish that live in the Atlantic, Pacific, and Indian oceans. They have a long spear-like bill. They are very fast swimmers on the hunt for food. Start at the ☆ to help this blue marlin find something to eat.

FINISH

See pages 66–69 for the answer key!

A seahorse has a long snout to suck tiny creatures into its mouth.

SPECTACULAR SPONGES

Sponges look like plants but are animals that live on rocks or coral. There are over 5,000 kinds of them, big and small. There are **8** differences between these pictures of sponges. Can you find them all?

See pages 66–69 for the answer key!

A sea snake is a reptile. Its nostrils close when it is underwater.

This animal lives around the cold ocean waters of Antarctica. They are only two or three feet tall, which is about the height of a two-year-old boy or girl. Start at 1 and connect the dots to find out what animal this is.

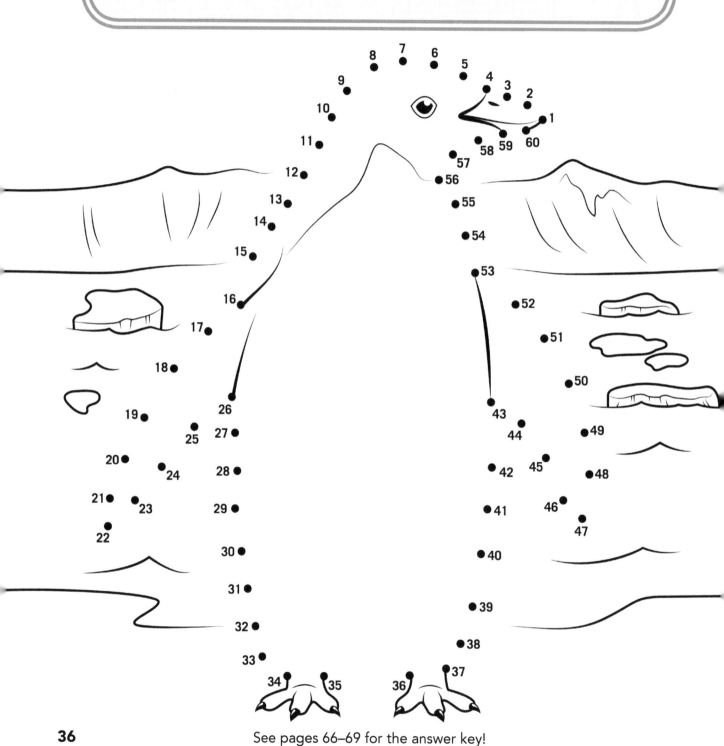

See pages 66–69 for the answer key!

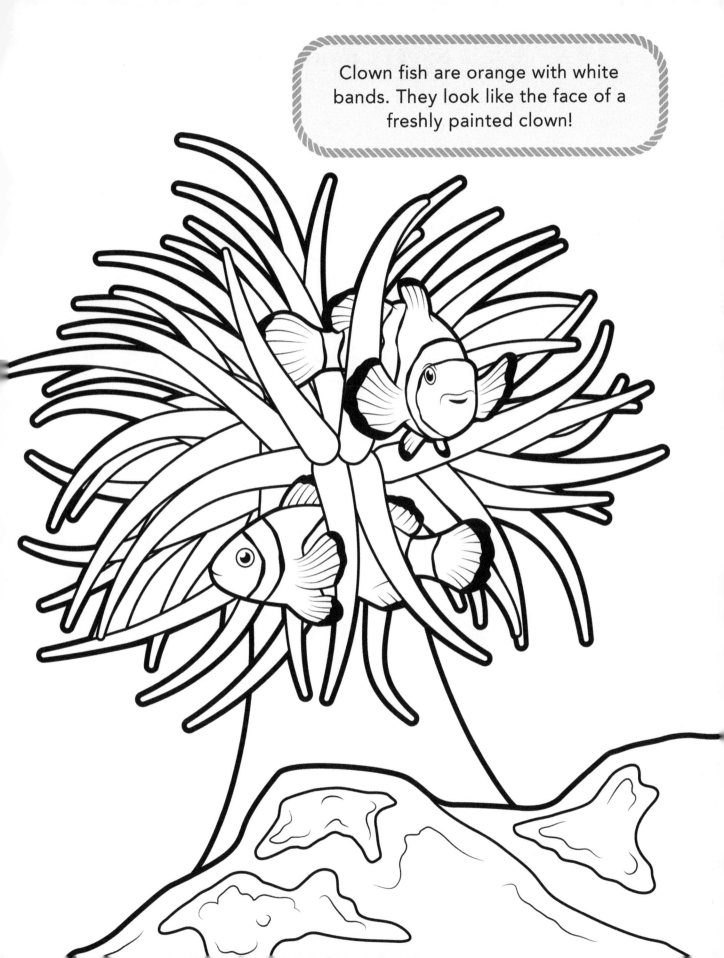

Clown fish are orange with white bands. They look like the face of a freshly painted clown!

SHELLS PROTECT

Some sea creatures have a hard shell on their body. The shell helps to protect them from other animals and sometimes the sun. Can you find these sea animals with shells hidden in the puzzle? Look left to right, right to left, up and down, and diagonally.

Hermit Crab
Clam
Lobster
Scallop

Shrimp
Krill
Sea Snail

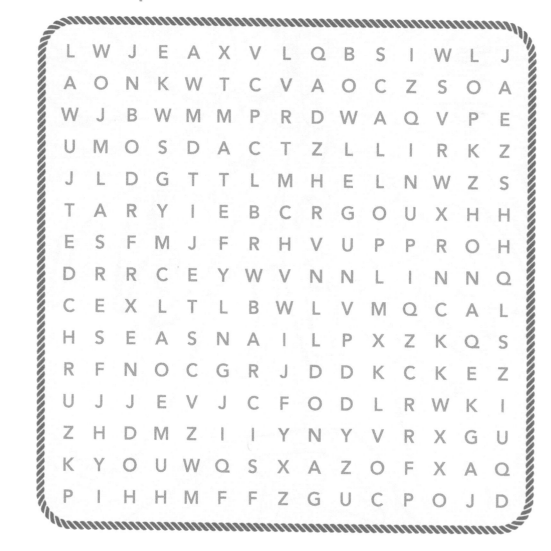

L W J E A X V L Q B S I W L J
A O N K W T C V A O C Z S O A
W J B W M M P R D W A Q V P E
U M O S D A C T Z L L I R K Z
J L D G T T L M H E L N W Z S
T A R Y I E B C R G O U X H H
E S F M J F R H V U P P R O H
D R R C E Y W V N N L I N N Q
C E X L T L B W L V M Q C A L
H S E A S N A I L P X Z K Q S
R F N O C G R J D D K C K E Z
U J J E V J C F O D L R W K I
Z H D M Z I I Y N Y V R X G U
K Y O U W Q S X A Z O F X A Q
P I H H M F F Z G U C P O J D

A crab walks sideways down the beach.

KELP HELP

A mother sea otter gives birth to one baby at a time called a "pup." The mother swims down in the ocean in search of food. To keep her pup from floating away while she's gone, she ties her baby in kelp. Start at the ⭐ to help the mother otter find clams for her pup.

FINISH

See pages 66–69 for the answer key!

A jellyfish looks like an umbrella
and is made mostly of water.

TIME FOR SCHOOL

A group of fish that swim together is called a "school" of fish. One reason they swim in a school is to make themselves look like a single big fish so they will not be eaten! There are **6** differences between these schools of fish. Can you find them all?

See pages 66–69 for the answer key!

A squid is a strong swimmer and moves quickly through the water tailfirst instead of headfirst.

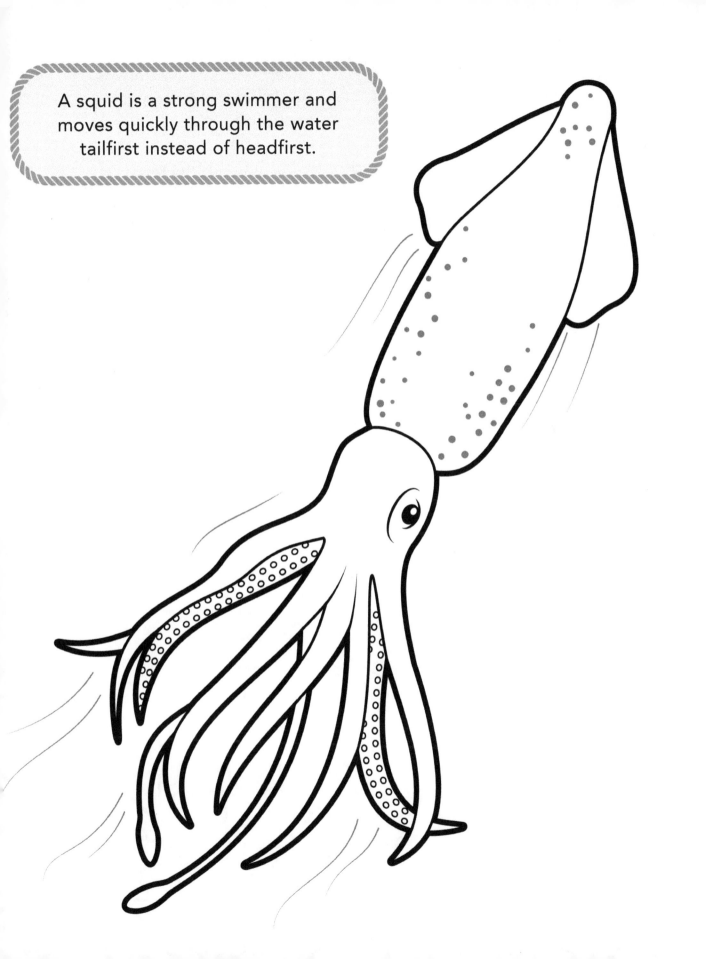

These fish are bright and colorful and live in warm tropical water. You can find them swimming around coral reefs. Start at 1 and connect the dots to find out what animal this is.

See pages 66–69 for the answer key!

A stingray does not have bones. It has cartilage like the tip of your nose.

WITHOUT A BACKBONE

Some sea animals do not have backbones. They are called "invertebrates." They can live in coral reefs, sea caves, and in both the shallow and deep parts of the ocean. Can you find the marine invertebrates hidden in the puzzle? Look left to right, right to left, up and down, and diagonally.

Sponges
Squid
Jellyfish

Octopus
Horseshoe Crab
Mussel

See pages 66–69 for the answer key!

Parrotfish help our coral reefs by eating the algae on them.

HUNGRY PUFFLING

Atlantic puffins can fly as well as swim. Puffins make a nest on the shore with grasses and feathers. A baby puffin is called a "puffling" and eats so much fish that both parents must bring it food! Start at the ☆ to help the mother and father find fish for their puffling.

FINISH

See pages 66–69 for the answer key!

A pelican has a pouch under its long bill to scoop up food from the water.

TIDE POOL TREASURES

When the tide moves back out to sea and leaves a pool of water, it is called a "tide pool." Different plants and animals live there. There are **6** differences between these tide pools. Can you find them all?

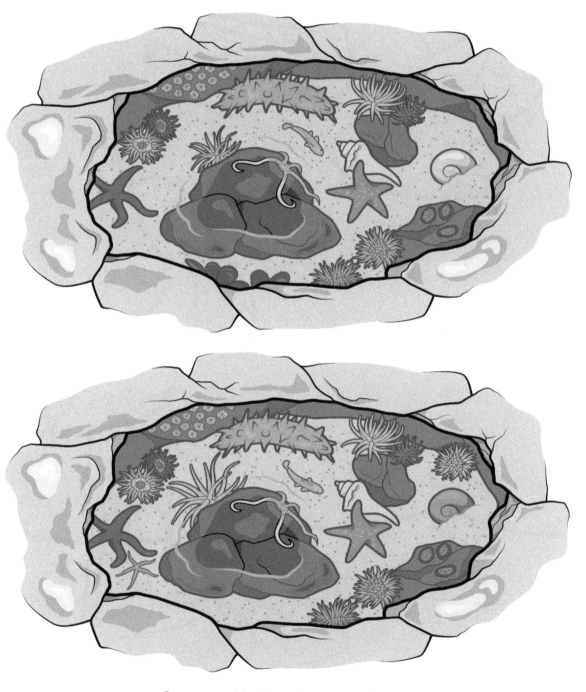

See pages 66–69 for the answer key!

The largest pearl in the world was made by a giant clam.

This animal lives in the Arctic Ocean. The mother gives birth to one baby at a time. A baby is called a "calf" and drinks milk from its mother. Start at 1 and connect the dots to find out what animals these are.

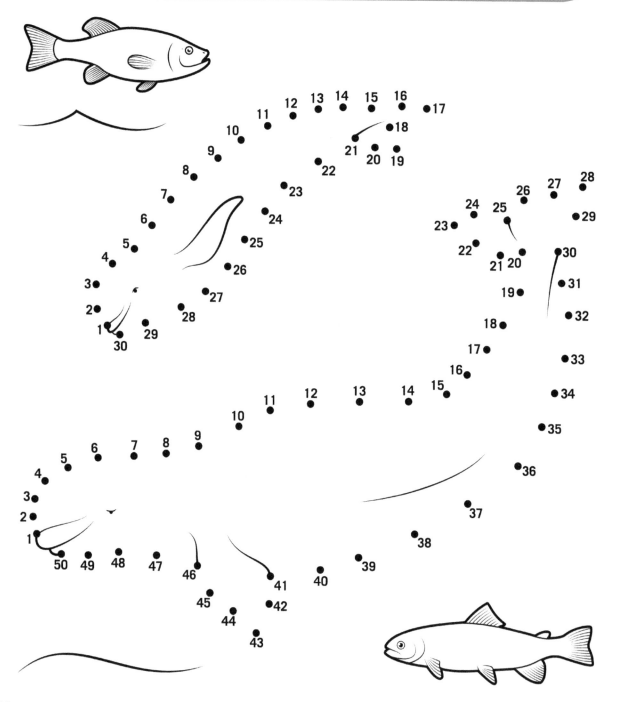

52

See pages 66–69 for the answer key!

A walrus uses its tusks to get food and climb onto ice.

FIVE OCEANS

An ocean is a body of water. Our Earth has five oceans that are all connected. Parts of the ocean are shallow, and parts are very deep. Can you find the five oceans of our Earth hidden in the puzzle? Look left to right, right to left, up and down, and diagonally.

Atlantic

Arctic

Pacific

Southern

Indian

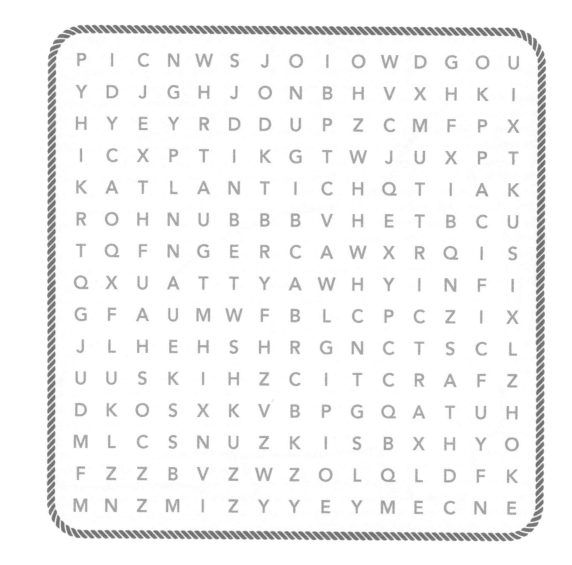

```
P I C N W S J O I O W D G O U
Y D J G H J O N B H V X H K I
H Y E Y R D D U P Z C M F P X
I C X P T I K G T W J U X P T
K A T L A N T I C H Q T I A K
R O H N U B B B V H E T B C U
T Q F N G E R C A W X R Q I S
Q X U A T T Y A W H Y I N F I
G F A U M W F B L C P C Z I X
J L H E H S R G N C T S C L
U U S K I H Z C I T C R A F Z
D K O S X K V B P G Q A T U H
M L C S N U Z K I S B X H Y O
F Z Z B V Z W Z O L Q L D F K
M N Z M I Z Y Y E Y M E C N E
```

See pages 66–69 for the answer key!

Another name for a manatee is a "sea cow." They are herbivores, which means they eat only plants.

THE SALMON RUN

The "salmon run" is a time when salmon leave the ocean and swim back up to the river. When they reach the river, they spawn, or lay eggs. Start at ⭐ to help the salmon go up the river to lay its eggs.

FINISH

See pages 66–69 for the answer key!

A sea anemone looks like a flower and attaches itself to rocks or coral.

WHALES BREACHING

Breaching is when a whale leaps out of the water. Scientists are not certain why whales breach, but they guess it may be to communicate or play. There are **6** differences between these breaching whales. Can you find them all?

See pages 66–69 for the answer key!

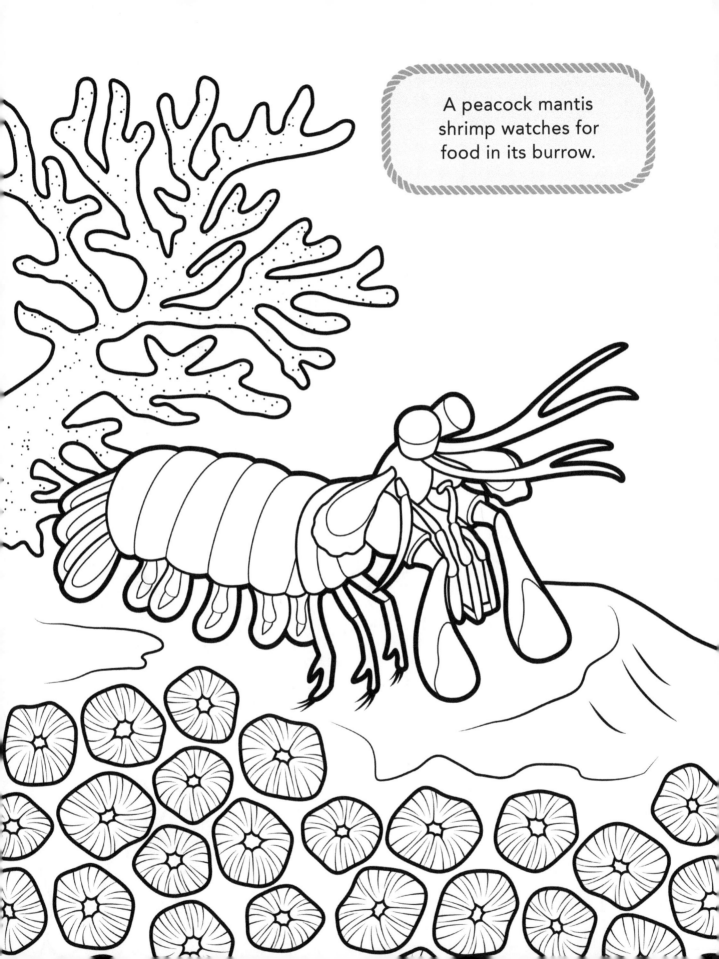

A peacock mantis shrimp watches for food in its burrow.

This fish looks like it wears pajamas. It is very social and likes to swim in groups. It has spots and lives in the Indian and Pacific oceans. Start at 1 and connect the dots to find out what animal this is.

See pages 66–69 for the answer key!

If a horseshoe crab flips over on the beach, it uses its tail, or "telson," to turn itself back over.

WHERE'S MY SCHOOL?

Yellow tang fish live in shallow water in the Indian and Pacific oceans. One yellow tang fish got lost in the reef. Start at the ☆ to help him find his way back to his school.

FINISH

See pages 66–69 for the answer key!

The sailfish is the fastest fish in the deep blue sea.

HERBIVORES ARE HELPFUL

Plant-eating marine animals are called "herbivores." They help keep the ocean clean by eating algae, seaweed, seagrasses, and other ocean plants. Can you find the marine herbivores hidden in the puzzle? Look left to right, right to left, up and down, and diagonally.

Manatee

Dugong

Parrotfish

Green Sea Turtle

Unicorn Fish

See pages 66–69 for the answer key!

Orcas are sometimes called "killer whales," but they are not whales at all—they're a type of dolphin.

ANSWER KEY

ALL KINDS OF SHARKS

Many kinds of sharks swim in the oceans of our world. They come in different sizes, shapes, and colors. Sharks have amazing senses that help them track their prey. Can you find these sharks hidden in the puzzle? Look left to right, right to left, up and down, and diagonally.

Great White
Tiger Shark
Whale Shark

Hammerhead
Bull Shark
Nurse Shark

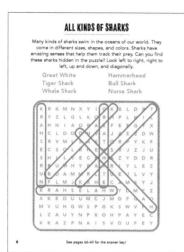

6   See pages 66–69 for the answer key!

HUMPBACK WHALE'S A-MAZE-ING JOURNEY!

In the fall, humpback whales leave the cold waters of Alaska and swim to the warmer waters in Hawaii. They swim almost nonstop for several weeks. Help the humpback whale find the way to warmer water. Start at the   near Alaska and follow the maze to finish in Hawaii.

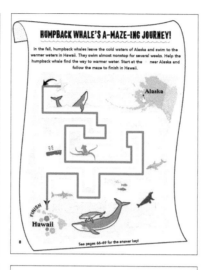

8   See pages 66–69 for the answer key!

EXPLORE THE CORAL REEF

Many ocean animals swim in and around coral reefs. Most coral reefs grow in shallow waters in the ocean. You will find amazing animals under the water. There are 8 differences between these coral reef pictures. Can you find them all?

10   See pages 66–69 for the answer key!

This animal is called the "Unicorn of the Sea" because of the long tusk that sticks out of its head. Start at 1 and connect the dots to find out what animal this is.

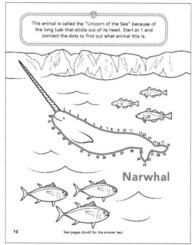

Narwhal

12   See pages 66–69 for the answer key!

MARINE MAMMALS

Marine mammals have fur or hair, breathe air, and are warm-blooded. They also have live babies and feed them with milk. These things make them different from fish. Can you find these marine mammals? Look left to right, right to left, up and down, and diagonally.

Whale
Walrus
Manatee
Dolphin

Otter
Seal
Polar Bear
Porpoise

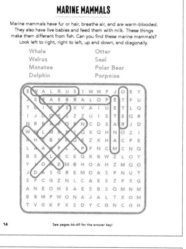

14   See pages 66–69 for the answer key!

SEA TURTLE SCRAMBLE

Mother sea turtles dig nests on the beach to lay their eggs. Baby sea turtles called "hatchlings" come out of the eggs. At night they leave their nests and crawl to the ocean. Start at the   to help the baby sea turtles crawl from their sandy nests to the ocean waves.

16   See pages 66–69 for the answer key!

SEA LION COLONIES

Sea lions live in the ocean and on land. They like to rest together in groups called "colonies." Many times, you will find them soaking up the sun on rocks or swimming in the ocean together. There are 6 differences between these sea lion colonies. Can you find them all?

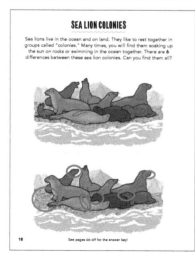

18   See pages 66–69 for the answer key!

This fish has slime on its skin to keep from getting cut or hurt on rocks. Start at 1 and connect the dots to find out what animal this is.

Eel

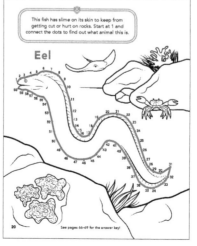

20   See pages 66–69 for the answer key!

SINGING WHALES

Did you know that some whales can sing? They call to one another under the water. It sounds just like a song! Can you find these whales hidden in the puzzle? Look left to right, right to left, up and down, and diagonally.

Beluga
Gray Whale
Sperm Whale

Blue Whale
Humpback

22   See pages 66–69 for the answer key!

HERMIT CRAB'S HOME

A hermit crab finds a hard, empty shell for protection and shelter. As it grows, it swaps the smaller shell for a bigger one. Start at the ☆ to help this hermit crab find a bigger shell.

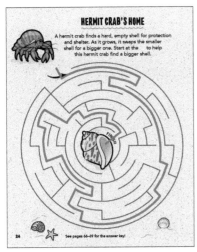

24   See pages 66–69 for the answer key!

AN ENDANGERED OCEAN ANIMAL

The short-tailed albatross is in danger of becoming extinct. There are only around 2,200 left. Today their habitat is protected to help keep them safe. There are **5** differences between these pictures of short-tailed albatrosses. Can you find them all?

26   See pages 66–69 for the answer key!

This animal is an excellent fast swimmer. It has a long body that looks like a torpedo. Start at 1 and connect the dots to reveal the animals below.

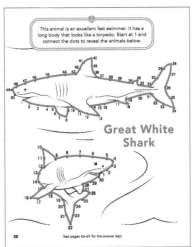

Great White Shark

28   See pages 66–69 for the answer key!

SAILING SEABIRDS

Seabirds eat fish and can drink salt water. They have two special glands on their heads to help get rid of the salt from the ocean water. Can you find these seabirds hidden in the puzzle? Look left to right, right to left, up and down, and diagonally.

Albatross   Seagull
Puffin   Loon
Penguin   Tern
Pelican   Murre

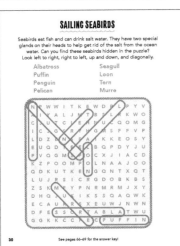

30   See pages 66–69 for the answer key!

FEEDING FRENZY

Blue marlin are fish that live in the Atlantic, Pacific, and Indian oceans. They have a long spear-like bill. They are very fast swimmers on the hunt for food. Start at the ☆ to help this blue marlin find something to eat.

32   See pages 66–69 for the answer key!

SPECTACULAR SPONGES

Sponges look like plants but are animals that live on rocks or coral. There are over 5,000 kinds of them, big and small. There are **8** differences between these pictures of sponges. Can you find them all?

34   See pages 66–69 for the answer key!

This animal lives around the cold ocean waters of Antarctica. They are only two or three feet tall, which is about the height of a two-year-old boy or girl. Start at 1 and connect the dots to find out what animal this is.

Adelie Penguin

36   See pages 66–69 for the answer key!

SHELLS PROTECT

Some sea creatures have a hard shell on their body. The shell helps to protect them from other animals and sometimes the sun. Can you find these sea animals with shells hidden in the puzzle? Look left to right, right to left, up and down, and diagonally.

Hermit Crab   Shrimp
Clam   Krill
Lobster   Sea Snail
Scallop

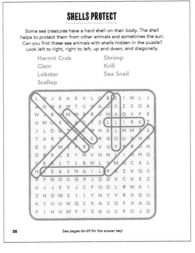

38   See pages 66–69 for the answer key!

KELP HELP

A mother sea otter gives birth to one baby at a time called a "pup." The mother swims down in the ocean in search of food. To keep her pup from floating away while she's gone, she ties her baby in kelp. Start at the ☆ to help the mother otter find clams for her pup.

40   See pages 66–69 for the answer key!

TIME FOR SCHOOL

A group of fish that swim together is called a "school" of fish. One reason they swim in a school is to make themselves look like a single big fish so they will not be eaten! There are **6** differences between these schools of fish. Can you find them all?

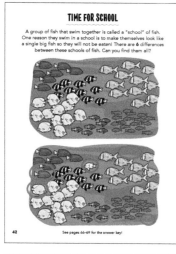

See pages 66–69 for the answer key!

These fish are bright and colorful and live in warm tropical water. You can find them swimming around coral reefs. Start at 1 and connect the dots to find out what animal this is.

Angelfish

See pages 66–69 for the answer key!

WITHOUT A BACKBONE

Some sea animals do not have backbones. They are called "invertebrates." They can live in coral reefs, sea caves, and in both the shallow and deep parts of the ocean. Can you find the marine invertebrates hidden in the puzzle? Look left to right, right to left, up and down, and diagonally.

Sponges   Octopus
Squid   Horseshoe Crab
Jellyfish   Mussel

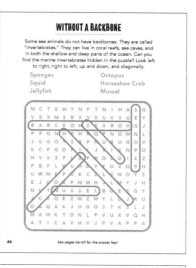

See pages 66–69 for the answer key!

HUNGRY PUFFLING

Atlantic puffins can fly as well as swim. Puffins make a nest on the shore with grasses and feathers. A baby puffin is called a "puffling" and eats so much fish that both parents must bring it food! Start at the ⬤ to help the mother and father find fish for their puffling.

See pages 66–69 for the answer key!
FINISH

TIDE POOL TREASURES

When the tide moves back out to sea and leaves a pool of water, it is called a "tide pool." Different plants and animals live there. There are **6** differences between these tide pools. Can you find them all?

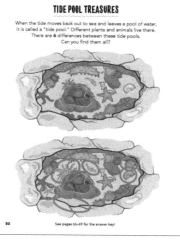

See pages 66–69 for the answer key!

This animal lives in the Arctic Ocean. The mother gives birth to one baby at a time. A baby is called a "calf" and drinks milk from its mother. Start at 1 and connect the dots to find out what animals are below.

Beluga Whale

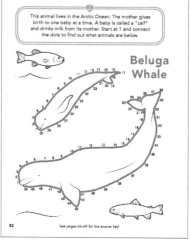

See pages 66–69 for the answer key!

FIVE OCEANS

An ocean is a body of water. Our Earth has five oceans that are all connected. Parts of the ocean are shallow, and parts are very deep. Can you find the five oceans of our Earth hidden in the puzzle? Look left to right, right to left, up and down, and diagonally.

Atlantic   Arctic
Pacific   Southern
Indian

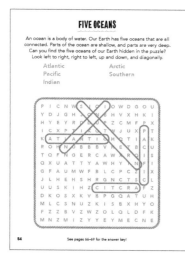

See pages 66–69 for the answer key!

THE SALMON RUN

The "salmon run" is a time when salmon leave the ocean and swim back up to the river. When they reach the river, they spawn, or lay eggs. Start at ⬤ to help the salmon go up the river to lay its eggs.

See pages 66–69 for the answer key!

WHALES BREACHING

Breaching is when a whale leaps out of the water. Scientists are not certain why whales breach, but they guess it may be to communicate or play. There are **6** differences between these breaching whales. Can you find them all?

See pages 66–69 for the answer key!

This fish looks like it wears pajamas. It is very social and likes to swim in groups. It has spots and lives in the Indian and Pacific oceans. Start at 1 and connect the dots to find out what animal this is.

Pajama Cardinalfish

See pages 66–69 for the answer key!

WHERE'S MY SCHOOL?

Yellow tang fish live in shallow water in the Indian and Pacific oceans. One yellow tang fish got lost in the reef. Start at the ★ to help him find his way back to his school.

See pages 66–69 for the answer key!

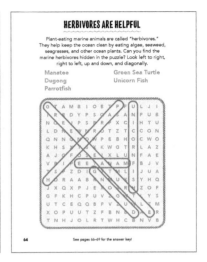

HERBIVORES ARE HELPFUL

Plant-eating marine animals are called "herbivores." They help keep the ocean clean by eating algae, seaweed, seagrasses, and other ocean plants. Can you find the marine herbivores hidden in the puzzle? Look left to right, right to left, up and down, and diagonally.

Manatee
Dugong
Parrotfish

Green Sea Turtle
Unicorn Fish

See pages 66–69 for the answer key!

ABOUT THE AUTHOR

 **Jill Richardson**'s passion is early childhood education. She has been an elementary teacher in Charlotte, North Carolina, for more than thirty years.

ABOUT THE ILLUSTRATOR

Kate Francis has illustrated many books ranging in topics from puppy training to horse sense, but this is her first activity book (and the most fun to draw). Her nieces and nephews helped her draw the mazes in this book. She lives in Austin, Texas, and can be found online at brownbirddesign.com.

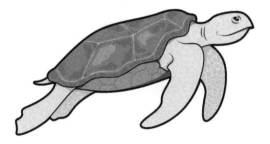

Copyright © 2020 by Rockridge Press, Emeryville, California

No part of this publication may be reproduced, stored in a retrieval system or transmitted in any form or by any means, electronic, mechanical, photocopying, recording, scanning or otherwise, except as permitted under Sections 107 or 108 of the 1976 United States Copyright Act, without the prior written permission of the Publisher. Requests to the Publisher for permission should be addressed to the Permissions Department, Rockridge Press, 6005 Shellmound Street, Suite 175, Emeryville, CA, 94608.

Limit of Liability/Disclaimer of Warranty: The Publisher and the author make no representations or warranties with respect to the accuracy or completeness of the contents of this work and specifically disclaim all warranties, including without limitation warranties of fitness for a particular purpose. No warranty may be created or extended by sales or promotional materials. The advice and strategies contained herein may not be suitable for every situation. This work is sold with the understanding that the Publisher is not engaged in rendering medical, legal, or other professional advice or ser-vices. If professional assistance is required, the services of a competent professional person should be sought. Neither the Publisher nor the author shall be liable for damages arising herefrom. The fact that an individual, organization or website is referred to in this work as a citation and/or potential source of further information does not mean that the author or the Publisher endorses the informa-tion the individual, organization or website may provide or recommendations they/it may make. Further, readers should be aware that Internet websites listed in this work may have changed or disappeared between when this work was written and when it is read.

For general information on our other products and services or to obtain technical support, please contact our Customer Care Department within the U.S. at (866) 744-2665, or outside the U.S. at (510) 253-0500.

Rockridge Press publishes its books in a variety of electronic and print formats. Some content that appears in print may not be available in electronic books, and vice versa.

TRADEMARKS: Rockridge Press and the Rockridge Press logo are trademarks or registered trade-marks of Callisto Media Inc. and/or its affiliates, in the United States and other countries, and may not be used without written permission. All other trademarks are the property of their respective owners. Rockridge Press is not associated with any product or vendor mentioned in this book.

Art Manager: Samantha Ulban
Editor: Eliza Kirby
Production Editor: Ashley Polikoff
Author photo © Tom Scherer of Queen City Media
Illustrations: © 2020 Kate Francis. All Other Art Courtesy of Shutterstock.

ISBN: 978-1-64611-691-1
R0

CPSIA information can be obtained
at www.ICGtesting.com
Printed in the USA
BVHW021015130320
574788BV00004B/1